ARISE

A Guided Journal to Help You Change Careers

ARISE

A Guided Journal to Help You Change Careers

Copyright © 2020 by Innovation Consultants of DeKalb. Written by Shermaine Perry.

ISBN: 979-8649900508

All rights reserved. No part of this book may be used or reproduced in any manner whatsoever without the prior written permission of the author.

Dedication

I dedicate this book to my mother Hermine Hinds-Perry, my siblings Kirwin, Shanita, and Shandra, and my husband André. Everyone needs a brainstorming team, cheering squad, and supporters like mine.

With Love,

Shermaine Perry

Sections

Introduction

Passion

Purpose

Prepare

Position

Play

Proficiency

Mentor

Innovate

Introduction

I created this journal to inspire others so that you can change careers even when you don't know where to start.

You will learn more about yourself, start the heavy lifting, and create a winning strategy with confidence on the journey to a new career.

This book is meant for everyday use. It should be used in consecutive order. You can spend as much time as needed on each section.

Shermaine Perry

Passion

A strong liking or desire for or devotion to some activity, object, or concept

Passion is critically important to happiness. It gives you a reason to keep learning and growing. Passion sparks curiosity and the desire for new experiences. It is that pull that feeds persistence and lights the path of success. Use this section to rediscover your passion.

Return to this page after completing this section.

What did you learn about yourself? Share one thing that you plan to do differently.

_____

_____

_____

_____

Passion

What activities did you love to do as a kid?

_____
_____
_____
_____
_____
_____
_____
_____
_____
_____
_____
_____
_____
_____
_____
_____
_____
_____
_____

Passion

What can you talk about for hours that when you talk about it, you light up?

_____
_____
_____
_____
_____
_____
_____
_____
_____
_____
_____
_____
_____
_____
_____
_____
_____
_____

Passion

If you were financially secure, what would you do with your time?

_____
_____
_____
_____
_____
_____
_____
_____
_____
_____
_____
_____
_____
_____
_____
_____
_____

Passion

What do you find fulfilling, meaningful, enjoyable, and important?

_____
_____
_____
_____
_____
_____
_____
_____
_____
_____
_____
_____
_____
_____
_____
_____
_____
_____
_____
_____

Passion

What were you passionate about as a child?

_____
_____
_____
_____
_____
_____
_____
_____
_____
_____
_____
_____
_____
_____
_____
_____
_____
_____
_____
_____

Passion

What did you want to be when you were 10 years old?

_____
_____
_____
_____
_____
_____
_____
_____
_____
_____
_____
_____
_____
_____
_____
_____
_____
_____
_____
_____

Passion

What hobbies did you enjoy as a teenager, but no longer do?

Passion

What is one dream that you tucked away for now?

Purpose

What is your "WHY"?

Knowing your purpose in life helps you live life with confidence and integrity. People who know their purpose in life know who they are, what they are, and why they are. When you know yourself, it becomes easier to find a career that's true to your core values. Use this section to discover your purpose.

Return to this page after completing this section.

What did you learn about yourself? Share one thing that you plan to do differently.

_____

_____

_____

_____

Purpose

What is the most rewarding thing you've ever done for someone else?

Purpose

Why was it rewarding?

Purpose

How do others describe your impact on their lives? Ask a few friends and family members.

Purpose

If you had all the time in the world to volunteer, who would you volunteer for?

_____
_____
_____
_____
_____
_____
_____
_____
_____
_____
_____
_____
_____
_____
_____
_____
_____
_____
_____
_____

Purpose

What groups or causes are really important to you?

_____
_____
_____
_____
_____
_____
_____
_____
_____
_____
_____
_____
_____
_____
_____
_____
_____
_____
_____
_____

Purpose

What moments in your life have been the hardest? Often these challenging moments create purpose.

Purpose

When you look back over the years, what are you most proud of?

Prepare

See yourself

A job is about duties but a career change is about growth. Take a step back and observe yourself as a professional. Get to know your strengths and areas in need of improvement. Then, look for ways to build on those strengths, and seek out opportunities to add to your skill set. Use this section to prepare for the next career move.

Return to this page after completing this section.

What did you learn about yourself? Share one thing that you plan to do differently.

_____

_____

_____

_____

Prepare

Why do you want to change jobs? Be honest with yourself.

Prepare

What do you know about the career you want? Take 10 minutes to list everything.

Prepare

Why do you think you'll be successful in this new career?

___
___
___
___
___
___
___
___
___
___
___
___
___
___
___
___
___
___
___

Prepare

Is there anything common with my current role and the one that I am currently seeking? List everything

Prepare

How do you feel about starting fresh again? Keep in mind that your next role may require that you take direction from a senior teammember who is younger in age.

Prepare

What is the best thing you have learned from a former supervisor?

Prepare

What is the best professional compliment that you have ever received?

Prepare

What would you miss most if you were no longer in this current position? What do you like about it?

Position

Position yourself for career advancement.

Timing is everything. You have to be ready when an opportunity presents itself. Conduct research to build familiarity with the new career. Use this section to learn about the required skills and explore the impact of this career change.

Return to this page after completing this section.

What did you learn about yourself? Share one thing that you plan to do differently.

_____

_____

_____

_____

Position

What do you know about the target career? Take 10 minutes to list everything.

_____
_____
_____
_____
_____
_____
_____
_____
_____
_____
_____
_____
_____
_____
_____
_____
_____
_____
_____
_____

Position

Which skills have you acquired in previous position that make you competitive in the job market?

Position

What specific job titles are most interesting to you? Chose one job title to research a current vacancy.

Position

Why are those job titles interesting?

Position

What aspects of these job titles do others dislike?

Position

On a scale of 1 to 10, ten being "I am a perfect technical match for (choose one) current vacancy", where would you rate yourself?

Position

If less than an eight, take three deep breaths. Write down how you feel about it? This guide will help uncover and build those missing skills.

_____
_____
_____
_____
_____
_____
_____
_____
_____
_____
_____
_____
_____
_____
_____
_____
_____
_____
_____

Position

"Who do I know that can connect me with opportunities in the career? Do not dismiss the knowledge of family, friends, and professional connections.

Position

What groups can connect me with opportunities in the career? Embrace connections made in affinity groups, religious groups, meetups, and Greek organizations.

Position

What do you value most: free time, recognition, or money?

Position

Are you ready to "dive in"?

Play

Dive in.

Jeff Besos says "the willingness to experiment is the key to doing new things". It is important to explore different aspects of a potential career and to allow curiosity to give a 360 view. Every opportunity has challenges and rewards. Fail forward and hear stories of lessons learned. Use this section to dive in and create familiarity within.

Return to this page after completing this section.

What did you learn about yourself? Share one thing that you plan to do differently.

_____

_____

_____

_____

Play

Where do you want to start? Revisit that current job vacancy.

Play

How do you spend a typical day? List everything hour by hour.

Play

How do you spend a typical day? List everything hour by hour.

Play

Block out at least an hour for deliberate learning each day to master a new skill. How will you find time to learn something new?

_____
_____
_____
_____
_____
_____
_____
_____
_____
_____
_____
_____
_____
_____
_____
_____
_____
_____
_____
_____

Play

What skill do you want to build/grow first? Why?

Play

What opportunities can help you get that skill? See value in every opportunity.

Play

What did you do today that helped you grow a new skill? This can be a networking conversation, research on a membership website, or reading a book.

Play

What does the new career have that my current one does not?

Play

Are you ready to do the heavy lifting? How bad do you want this career change?

Play

List the skills, interest, and talents needed for the new position.

Play

What long-term opportunities are associated with this new career?

Play

What's the potential for promotion? Perhaps it will take many years of experience to secure a supervisory position in this career path.

Play

What obstacles do you have to face while making this career transition? Other than the necessary qualifications required (Think about time with family, money, etc.).

Play

How can you minimize the struggles that you predicted?

_____
_____
_____
_____
_____
_____
_____
_____
_____
_____
_____
_____
_____
_____
_____
_____
_____
_____
_____
_____

Play

What do you hope to gain from this new career?

Play

Are you being realistic? How are you feeling about this?

Proficiency

Master skills to set yourself apart.

By taking the initiative in your own career development and actively working to display your skills
in your current job, you'll find that you're much better equipped to advance when the next promotional opportunity arises. Use this section to create value.

Return to this page after completing this section.

What did you learn about yourself? Share one thing that you plan to do differently.

_____

_____

_____

_____

Proficiency

What skills do you want to build? Why?

Proficiency

What skills do you need to build? Why?

Proficiency

What opportunities can help you get that skill? See value in every opportunity.

Proficiency

Choose one skill from the previous page. Write it below.

Proficiency

Who can mentor you to gain this skill?

Proficiency

What books can help you grow this skill? List 3 books.

Proficiency

What YouTube videos can help you grow this skill? List 3 videos.

Proficiency

What digital resources can help you grow this skill? List 3 free digital resources from our local library system.

Proficiency

What LinkedIn courses can help you grow this skill? List 3 courses.

Proficiency

Are you ready to show what you know? Consult on a project with your mentor to gain experience with this skill.

Mentor

Consult, counsel, and encourage others.

Mentorship is about finding ways to share your knowledge, skills, and experience with less knowledgeable or less experienced people. It is important to help others develop professionally and personally. Give someone else an opportunity to learn from you. Use this section to learn more about yourself and the benefits of mentorship.

Return to this page after completing this section.

What did you learn about yourself? Share one thing that you plan to do differently.

_____

_____

_____

_____

Mentor

If you could sit down with your 15-year old self, what would you tell him or her about your career?

Mentor

What would you tell your 20-year old self about your journey as a professional in the working world?

_____
_____
_____
_____
_____
_____
_____
_____
_____
_____
_____
_____
_____
_____
_____
_____
_____
_____

Mentor

What are the two biggest lessons you learned from previous jobs?

Mentor

How can you use your experiences to help others?

Mentor

Are there parallels to what you chose as a career and what you loved as a child? How can you share this with younger professionals?

_____
_____
_____
_____
_____
_____
_____
_____
_____
_____
_____
_____
_____
_____
_____
_____
_____
_____
_____
_____

Innovate

Create your own path.

Innovation is at the heart of every passionate professional. Disrupt the traditional approach and try something different. Ask for feedback. Ask "why not" instead of "why". Creative problem solving techniques and cutting-edge ideas are on the tip of your tongue. Use this section to understand how innovation can impact your personal brand.

Return to this page after completing this section.

What did you learn about yourself? Share one thing that you plan to do differently.

_____

_____

_____

_____

Innovate

What is one thing what you are deeply proud of, but would never put on your resume?

Innovate

What are you amazingly good at? Create an ePortfolio to brand yourself.

Use what you learned to make that career change! It is work but it is worth it!

Bonus

Whatever you think you can't do, just know that there is someone who is confidently doing it wrong right now. They have no plans at doing it better either and people are paying them to do it. Please believe in your own excellence as much as they believe in their mediocrity.

Connect with us online

Amazon Author Page
amazon.com/author/shermaineperry

innovationconsultants.co

innovationconsultantsco

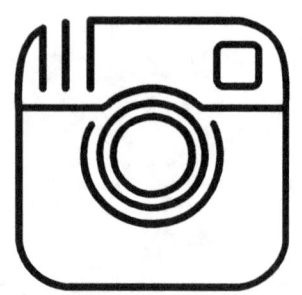

innovationconsultantsco

Like the Product?

WE ARE SO GLAD THAT YOU ARE HAPPY. SPREAD THE JOY BY:

- **a**   Sharing your experience on AMAZON by writing a review.
- 📱   Telling your friends and family about it.
- **f**   Post about it.

www.ingramcontent.com/pod-product-compliance
Lightning Source LLC
Chambersburg PA
CBHW081311070526
44578CB00006B/838